Poetry From The Desert Floor

Pat Kelley

Poetry from the Desert Floor

Copyright 2012 by Pat Kelley

All rights reserved

Photographs by Pat Kelley
Published by Kelley B Arts
Clinton, WA 98236

Library of Congress Cataloging
Kelley, Pat

Poetry from the desert floor

ISBN: 1470024799

ISBN 13: 9781470024796

741

Poetry
Desert Poetry

Preface

As a child, my dad and I hiked and fished the desert so I developed an early love affair with the distinctive biomes that survive successfully in an arid, mostly waterless, ecosystem. This book is dedicated to the people, places and things that live the mysteries of one of the most beautiful places on earth.

People

Growing Up Stinkweed

You aint gonna survive
Ridin that horse at breakneck speed.
There's potholes out there.
Lookit him, all lathered up and puffin.
You gonna kill your best friend.

Mom, I'll be better next time.
It's just that the wind gets in my hair
and I forget where I am and what I'm doing.
The spirit gets me
And I just have to go.

Wives and Mothers

Weathered hands reach into her apron pocket
staples and penetrating oil always ready
essentials of the desert-wife's life.
Oil the gates so the hinges don't squeak,
haul a rock to hold the fence
so the livestock can't escape
'til somebody fixes it,
feed the crew—family and the hired help,
summer and winter, three times a day
scrub the floors
carry the wood
milk the cows
occasionally drive a truck
raise the children
and stand at her husband's side
as he prays for rain and
resigns himself to the whims of the weather.

Woman of The Desert

She stands at the window
Nose pressed against the pane
Watching
Smiling
The rhythm of his boots
Clicks a greeting on the porch
Woman of the desert
Unclip your plaited hair
Let fall your cotton dress
The night is yours.

Home Run

Smack,
Ting
Ball colliding with bat.
Pounding to first
Richocheting off second,
Charging third,
Home run.
Ecstacy.

On the mound I
Pitch a perfect game-
A no-hitter.
We win!
Cheers from the guys.

Fast pitch: sorry, but you can't play.
Strike one.
What?
New rules, Little League rules
Girls might get hurt.
Strike two.
Baseball is for boys.
Strike tree
I'm out.
Foul ball.
Error in 1949.
Smack,
Ting

56 years later—2005
She is 11 years old
She pitches a no hitter
She bats 718
The guys cheer
The crowd goes wild.
Home run: Title IX.

Macho Men in Cowboy Boots

Macho men in cowboy boots
Living in pine country
Have a ritual.
When they get a new snowmobile
They drive it down the streets of town-
Past the general store, past the bar,
Past the one tank gas station
into old Bill John's field.
They shout, they holler.
they blow their horns.
They do this at midnight,
Firing rifles into the cold night air
Wreaking havoc on this tiny town.
Snow or no snow; doesn't matter.
Most go to the hospital
Broken legs and such.
Ken Jackson didn't need to die.

Lee

The grizzled cowboy sits at the bar
His faced etched in leather,
His gnarled hands lean and strong.
He speaks of his hard life
And shows me his belly
Riddled with holes from Vietnam.

Women who Built The Desert

Think of those women
raising children
sweeping floors
milking cows
living lives of seeming desolation.

Do not believe
their lives were led in quiet desperation
for they built the communities,
provided the backbone
and grit
that built the nation.

Uncle Harry's Spur Rides Pony Express

Uncle Harry's spur
Hangs on my wall
A relic of the
Short history of the
Pony Express.
A memento to the brave young men
Who rode hundreds of miles
Across deserts and mountains
To deliver the mail
From St. Joseph, Missouri
To San Francisco, California,
It knew a fresh horse every
Fifteen miles.
Hard on men
Harder on horses.
That old rowel gave up its
Place in history
To the telegraph
And then to the Iron Horse.

The Graduates

Ten students stand, receive diplomas
and say goodbye to the thirty-three others in their
high desert school.

Four go off to fight the war.
Two are twins.
The only paycheck they can imagine is war-
No jobs in their tiny town.

One returns to his Navajo village in Arizona
The father of two, unmarried,
An artist of exceptional talent.

Two are off to college
They go as sweethearts, promising an
Eternity of love and devotion.

The other two hang out around town.
One does odd jobs for the ranchers.

The other has a baby and moves off the
mountain to find work.

The tenth commits suicide on the
way home from the senior party
taking the turn at a hundred miles an hour,
hitting the tree in the yard where she baby sits.

Ten years later

The twins survive the war
The girl marries a black man and
brings him back to the desert
where neither is wanted or accepted.
Two children later,
they move to his home in Louisiana.

The boy re-ups twice. He likes the
paycheck and sees Iraq twice.
He'll re-up again and again
until he has his twenty years.

One fights ghosts in the mountains of
Afghanistan up near the Pakistani border.
He lost several of his buddies.
He's been there four years and
wants to come home--
but they won't let him.

The other joined the navy
was first stationed in Hawaii,
and then in San Diego.
He calls home often.
He married a beautiful girl from San Diego.

The artist lives in a hut in the
Arizona desert with his mother
without running water or electricity.
He paints when he wants to
and sells his work on the side of
the road to tourists who ooh
and ahh at his majestic Indian paintings.

College is not kind to one.
He drops out and returns to the valley
to work in the fields. They say he
Liked to drink and party more than study.

His love finishes college, finds
a great job in the big city, a new love.
The wedding is in the desert.

Odd jobs are hard to find in the valley
So the graduate moves to the river and learns
To run tugs. He gets his license,
marries a waitress and fathers a child.

The girl carries the baby off to school
And in two years gets an associate degree.
She tells the father to go to hell
And she and her daughter raise each other.

We knew you planned your leaving.
No matter how hard we talked to you,
tried to convince you that there was
a world beyond the valley,
beyond your family,
we knew you wouldn't stay.
Each grows into a desert bloom, fragile, beautiful, human.

Bikers

A hundred and fifty Harley motorcycles
Rumble up the school drive
Colors flying.

Gawkers watch,
Hesitant to even consider
What business a
Hundred and fifty bikers
Might have at this ceremony.

They drive up the hill
in formation-four abreast.

Why are they here?
What do they want?
Who do they want?

Dressed in black leathers
They enter the bleachers.

They are here to honor their leader's son
Who this day
Graduates with honors.

Sally's Song

For ten years my friend fought cancer.
First one breast
and then the other.
Today it's Melanoma.
An expert at treatments,
she knows the language
from biopsy and benign
to surgery and side effects.
Today her vocabulary contains only "M" words:
Mammogram, Malignant, Metastasize,
Mastectomy, Melanoma,
Motherfucker,
Meditation,
Marrow.
Mortal.

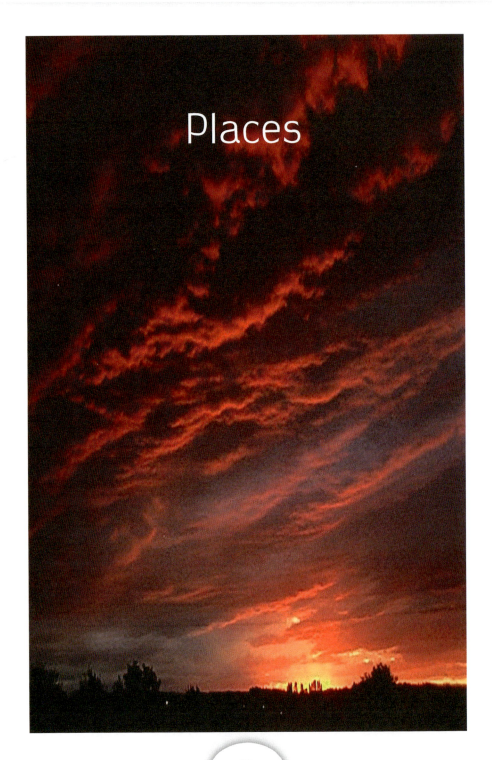

Old Houses

History reflects
shapes and sizes
even as they tumble to the ground.
Angled rooflines,
weathered wood,
ornate accessories,
once shaped these now bleak exteriors.
Like Ozymandias searching to be remembered,
tumbleweed suggests a hidden past.
What was the history?
Who lived, loved and died here?
Why was it abandoned to the
weather, insects and rodents?

I look and reminisce,
I too, am becoming a relic
and my history is at least as interesting.

Guardian of The Past

A ghost of the 40s and 50s,
an old gas station
stands abandoned in
desert dust and grime,
tumbleweed clogging doors
long closed and forgotten

An eyesore
in this neat and tidy town,
its two pumps stand sentry-like
guarding the past from the future
afraid that somehow
history will be lost
if its memory is removed

Morning

I sit in the smoky haze
Of a foggy spring morning
Sipping my coffee
Watching rabbits devour
Tender leaves
Resenting their cuteness
Wishing I had the courage
To shoot them
Knowing I will eventually
Buy hundreds of dollars
Of rabbit fencing
To keep them from my
Cauliflower and broccoli

The Rogue River Canyon

Gnarled oak branches draw puzzles
against deep blue skies.
Deer and mink forage for food
carefully avoiding white water that
tumbles and crashes from its
origins near Crater Lake.

Feathered in down jackets,
we drift the river in search of
Eagles displaying winter plumage:

The old house sits in a clearing,
pine trees circling it
like so many sentries
at an old fort
waiting for the enemy.
Stiletto pointed icicles hang
from the roof.
Blackberry vines encroach on a hundred
years of history.

Who lived here?
Zane Grey writing
"Rogue River Feud"?
or was it Dutch Henry,
mule skinner extraordinaire,
self-appointed assassin?

Why did they choose isolation over civilization?
What stories does the river hide?

Ghosts of The Desert

Wisps of fog rise from the desert
glazing the landscape of
muted greens and gold.
A lake emerges
flat and gray
its edges rimmed in white.
Rising from the water
a church spire stands
battered and chipped by desert winds
a monolith to history.

Is it, too, an illusion or
did conquistadors
once gather here
to worship?

Grand Canyon

I step to the rim
and view the layered history
of the world
its towering walls
eroded by wind and water
hiding ancient fossils
that mark our time.

I am awed.
A riot of color speaks to me
beckons to me to chance
a walk into the
raw, yawning vastness
before me.

Colors

Evening colors of the desert break purple and red
crowding out the dull brown canvas of daylight.

Against the glow
I look for the sentinels
tall Saguaros,
a Joshua tree,
stone sculpted by the wind-

These are my friends.

Ode to the Cascades

Up from the dessert floor
the giant dragon rises,
jagged spines lifting towards the sky,
a thousand ridges
seeking snow and sun.

Birds sit on your bones
warbling odes to your
scales of green and blue and gold
not knowing when you will
raise your mighty head
and drive them out.

Majestic and perilous
you are passive in your sleep
until offended.
Then the sky lights red
against the
darkness of rain and ash.

Around the Pacific
your friends slumber-
waiting their turn to eject
horror, and devastation.

Volcanic eruptions--
the building blocks of your beauty.

Fly Fishing in Watercolor

In the creek I seek the area where
Cold rushing water meets
A quiet pool,
Where light dances gold and silver
On the oranges, greens and
Browns of autumn.

The white barked Aspens glisten
Like slivers of ice
Against the dark blue shadows of
The pool.

I cast my line
Watching it snake yellow across
The water. I feel the tension and
Jerk up fast.

The trout leaps, his colors speckled
In the sunlight.

I reel him in and let him go.

Summer

The sun sears its path to noon
scorching the earth
sending lizards and bugs to seek
tiny shadows for safety.

Pocket gophers burrow low,
hiding their young
in communal daycare centers
until the sun goes down.

I, too, wait for the moon
for the coyote's song
for cool breezes to caress my face.

In the wind, I smell the sweet
perfumes of the desert floor.

Desert Grasses

Grasses ripple in August breezes
Golden heads bursting forth rich kernels

Wheat
Oats
Corn
Barley
Rice
Rye

Food for the world.

Desert Storm

Winds blow
off the Rockies
leaving dirt on the floor,
in the bed,
on the old flowered sofa,
settling softly on the dishes.

I cover food with dishtowels
pull clothes from the line
rub dust from my eyes
all the while
watching the gigantic black clouds rimmed
in white
predicting torrential rains.

I close the doors and windows,
herd the animals into the barn
the air feeling like a tornado
although I know it isn't.

The arroyos fill,
water gushing over the banks
spawning small yellow flowers
destined for an old porcelain vase.

I catch rain in buckets
to wash my hair and merge
the tantalizing smells
of sage brush and rain.

In a moment,
it is gone

Coyotes

Young coyotes come to my screen
lean and golden
chatting in high-pitched voices.
They must have been abandoned
by their parents or
missed having lunch with the cat next door.
I love hearing them close by,
love their ragged call,
and wish them good luck in this barren land.

The Santa Anas

This fragile earth
enveloped in a
thin film of shifting winds
holds me close.
Dear earth,
do not let me blow away.

Monsoons

In August
come clouds
following the path
of the Colorado River.

Lightning bolts
dance across the skies
crackling hot,
penetrating the earth.

Sometimes it rains
sometimes flowers bloom
sometimes little tufts of grass
reach skyward.

But mostly it mocks
the dry cracked earth
and steams its way
back into the sky.

Written on The Wind

Mustangs
descendents of Spanish kings
roam the prairies and hills
of the high mesa desert.

Heads held high,
the wind catches in ripples
through flowing manes.
Their hooves pound the prairie grasses
racing against time
and man's encroachment.

Sheltered foals navigate canyons
avoid coyotes, man and
dreaded captivity.

These wild horses represent
our last memories of the old west,
freedom, independence, survival.
Theirs is a story
written on the wind.

Sentries

Three-bladed sentries
stand at attention
atop a desert rock
humming wind melodies
a carbonless footprint
in the 21st century

YUCCA

A lone Yucca
stands guard
in the white sands
of New Mexico
amid vast beauty
and military secrets

Water Wars

Man and horse hunker against the wind.
The horse carefully picking his way.
The man, his collar pulled tight
Scans the landscape for signs of water, a spring.

Any moisture in an arid land

Precious water
Brought forth by hand pumps
From dirty wells dug shallow in the ground.
Ochre colored water oozing
From occasional windmills pumping water
For livestock, homes, ranches.

Sweet, thirst-quenching water

In his saddle scabbard, a rifle rests
to defend his right to water.
He and his neighbors battle over
Rivers, lakes, creeks, springs, and underground aquifers.

Men die for water.

Man and horse pass an old windmill,
Its face turned aside,
Dead.

His neighbor, the farmer, moved out
Leaving his home to the rodents and sage brush.
Leaving his garden to dry up
Leaving the land he loved-

Losing it all.

Wind on The Desert Floor

Hot sand blows in funnels across the desert floor
Twirling, fighting, clinging
Spitting its contents miles away from its origins
Burying life
Waiting for rain
Spring
Flowers

The Rufus Hummingbird

I bathed a jewel today
and it took my breath.
As I stood rooted,
hose in hand
an incandescent Ruby
flew into my spray.
Feathers fluffed
wings abuzz
he scattered refracted silver droplets.
Finished,
nose to nose,
he thanked me,
and soared into the deep cerulean sky
in a cloud of delicate sparks.

Sanctuary

I walk into the desert and
wrap my arms against the wind.

I watch the stars move across a crystal-clear sky
unobstructed by smog and man.

A yucca blooms white against
Green-brown sage.

Out here, for a moment, I escape the television-
that continuous reminder
of the frailties of man
in other times and other places.

It is here that I think about my children
the wonder of their lives
how they grew to be such fine people
raised outstanding children of their own.

It is here that I contemplate
my roads not taken
the what-ifs.

Acknowledgements

I gratefully acknowledge the assistance of Bea and Jack Rawls for a lifetime of kicking me along, Mimi Marshall for her sense of humor, Berdene Saul for going over and over desert pictures, Carrie Lewis for reading numerous rewrites, Kay Lewis for editing, and Dorothy Read and Margaret Bendet for constant encouragement.

A special thanks to my husband Bob Brunjes for traveling to take pictures and his computer expertise and to my children Michael Hardy and Kathleen Murphy and their spouses Trish and Mike, grandchildren Caitlin, Sean, Cameron and Fiona for continuous inspiration.

About the Author

Pat is a retired teacher, librarian and school administrator. She has a doctorate in Educational Leadership; Curriculum and Instruction. Her poetry has won honors from the Willamette Writers Association Conference, Washington State Poetry Association, and the Whidbey Island Writers Association. She taught speech and English at both the high school and college levels, and coached many students to state and national winnings in speech and debate.

Writing, gardening, photography, painting, and artistic quilting keep her busy.

Pat teaches workshops on the Art of Storytelling: Learn to Read Your Own Materials Aloud.

She may be contacted at kelley@kelleybarts.com

Made in the USA
Charleston, SC
09 February 2013